ITALIAN
CHRISTMAS
COOKBOOK

THIS BOOK BELONGS TO

_____

_____

TABLE OF CONTENTS

Italian Christmas Cookies

YIELDS: 3 dozen

Ingredients

FOR THE COOKIES:

- 2/3 cup of powdered sugar
- 1 stick unsalted butter, softened
- 2 tsp. vanilla extract
- 3/4 teaspoons almond extract
- 3 big eggs
- 2 1/2 c. all-purpose flour, plus more for dusting
- 2 tsp. baking powder
- 3/4 tsp. salt

FOR THE GLAZE:

- 2 cups of powdered sugar
- 3 tbsp. milk
- 1/2 tsp. vanilla extract
- Red and green Jimmy sprinkles were used for embellishment.

Instructions

cookies:

1. In the bowl of a stand mixer fitted with the paddle attachment, beat the sugar, butter, vanilla extract, and almond extract on medium speed for about 2 minutes, or until smooth and fluffy. Add the eggs and mix thoroughly. (The batter will appear to be distinct)

2. With mixer on low, add the flour, baking powder, and salt gradually. Beat until the dry ingredients are completely mixed. Chill the dough in the refrigerator 1 hour and four hours.

3. Preheat the oven to 350 degrees F. Form the dough into approximately 36 1-inch balls (dusting hands lightly with flour as needed) and place on two baking sheets lined with parchment paper, leaving at least 1-inch between each ball. Alternatively, roll each dough ball (lightly dusted with flour if necessary) into a 4-inch-long log and coil each piece into a mound.

4. Bake the cookie for until the bottoms are firm and gently browned. Transfer cookie to a cooling rack and allow them to cool completely for about 30 minutes.

For the glaze:

1. Whisk the powdered sugar, milk, and vanilla extract in a medium bowl. Sprinkle the Jimmy sprinkles on top of each cookie after dipping it in the glaze and allowing any excess to fall off. Allow the cookies to rest until the glaze has set, approximately 30 minutes.

Classic pizzelle recipe for Italian waffle cookies

Yield: 24 PIZZELLE COOKIES

Prep time: 10 MINUTES

Cook time: 15 MINUTES

Total time: 25 MINUTES

Ingredients

- 3 big eggs

- 3/4 cup sugar
- 1/2 cup melted and cooled butter
- 1 tablespoon pure vanilla extract
- 1 3/4 cups sifted all-purpose flour
- 2 tablespoons of baking powder required

Instructions

1. In a mixing bowl, beat the eggs and sugar for roughly 2 to 3 minutes until they are pale yellow and foamy.
2. While continuing to beat, gradually pour in the melted, cooled butter. Then, incorporate vanilla extract.
3. In a separate basin, combine the flour and baking powder. Fold dry ingredients into the wet components with a spatula until barely combined.
4. Bake one medium scoop of cookie dough (about 1 1/2 tablespoons) for each mold for 30 seconds or until golden brown. Remove with a wooden spatula and cool thoroughly on a cooling rack.
5. As desired, dust-cooled pizzelles with powdered sugar.

notes

variations:

1. chocolate pizzelle recipe — remove the vanilla and add three teaspoons of cocoa powder and one-fourth cup of sugar.

2. almond pizzelle recipe — replace the vanilla essence with 1 tablespoon of pure almond extract.

3. Reduce the pure vanilla extract to 1 teaspoon and add 2 teaspoons of finely grated lemon zest to the lemon pizzelle preparation.

4. classic anise pizzelle recipe — add 1/2 teaspoon anise seed

Italian Fig Cookies

Prep Time: 45 mins

Cook Time: 12 mins

Total Time: 3 hrs 57 mins

Yield: 36 cookies

Ingredients

For the dough:

- 1/2 cup unsalted cold butter (113g or 4oz)
- ¼ cup granulated sugar (55g)
- 1/4 cup of light brown sugar (56g)
- 1 big egg at room temperature
- 1 teaspoon vanilla extract
- 1 ¾ cups all-purpose flour (226g)
- ¼ teaspoon baking soda
- ½ teaspoon salt

To prepare the filling:

- 1 cup chopped dry Calimyrna or Mission figs with stems removed (6 or 7-ounce package)
- 1/2 cup finely sliced pitted dates (or substitute raisins if preferred)
- 1/2 cup freshly squeezed orange juice (about 1 orange) (4oz)
- 1/3 cup candied orange peel diced
- two teaspoons of powdered sugar
- 1 teaspoon lemon zest
- 1/4 teaspoon cinnamon powder

- 1/3 cup blanched almonds finely chopped
- 2 tablespoons heavy spiced rum or Grand Marnier orange liqueur

To prepare the lemon glaze:

- 1 cup of sifted powdered sugar (115g)
- 2 tablespoons freshly squeezed lemon juice (add more if needed for desired consistency)
- Sprinkles for embellishment if desired

Instructions

To make the bread dough:

1. In a large mixing basin, beat the butter with an electric mixer on medium-high speed until smooth and creamy, about 1 minute. Add granulated sugar and brown sugar and blend thoroughly. Add the egg and vanilla and mix until just combined. Scrape the bowl's sides and beat for a few seconds more. Whisk the flour, baking soda, and salt together. Incorporate the flour mixture into the dough in three increments while mixing low speed.

2. Shape each dough half into a tiny rectangle. Refrigerate the dough for at least three hours and up to one day under plastic wrap.

To cook the filling:

1. Combine the figs, dates, orange juice, candied orange peel, sugar, lemon zest, and cinnamon in a small saucepan. The mixture brought to a boil over medium-high heat. Reduce the heat to medium-low and simmer for 5 to 8 minutes, until the fruit is tender and thick, or until the fruit is soft and the mixture is thick. Remove from fire and stir in the blanched almonds and, if using, 2 tablespoons of Grand Marnier.

Set aside until room temperature is reached. Once cold, cover with plastic wrap until required.

2. To assemble and bake cookies, preheat the oven to 375 degrees F. Parchment-line a baking sheet. Before rolling out the dough, remove it from the refrigerator and allow it to rest for 10 to 15 minutes.

3. Place a 14-by-10-inch piece of wax or parchment paper on a clean work area. The paper is liberally dusted with flour. One portion of the dough rolled into a 10x8-inch rectangle. Each rectangle is divided into two 104-inch strips. Place a 1/4 of the filling in the middle of each strip (in a rounded mound). Before rolling the dough and filling into cylinders, REFRIGERATE the dough and filling as-is for 10 to 15 minutes.

4. Using parchment paper as a guide, fold one of the dough's long sides over the filling. Repeat on the opposite side to build a tube around the filling. The dough should slightly extend beyond the filling. Gently seal the perimeters.

5. Transfer the filled strips to the prepared baking sheet, seam side down, and lay them down. Bake for until browned lightly.

6. Remove from oven and immediately cut each strip diagonally into 1-inch pieces using a broad, thin knife. Transfer the cookies to a cooling rack.

7. To prepare the lemon glaze:

8. Powdered sugar and lemon juice should be smooth. Sprinkle colorful sprinkles on top of each cookie, if desired.

Recipe Notes

- You can find chopped candied orange peel in the grocery store department containing fruit cake ingredients.
- Grand Marnier is used in this recipe.

ITALIAN BUTTER COOKIES

Prep Time: 15 minutes

Cook Time: 15 minutes

Total Time: 75 minutes

Yield: 18 cookie sandwiches 1x

INGREDIENTS

- 1 1/4 cup all-purpose flour
- 1/2 teaspoon salt
- 1/2 cup (1 stick) softened unsalted butter
- 1/2 cup granulated sugar
- 1 teaspoon vanilla extract
- 1/2 teaspoon of almond flavor or extract
- Bring one big egg to room temperature
- 1/2 cup strawberry or raspberry preserves
- 4 ounces chopped semisweet chocolate or chocolate chips (melted)

INSTRUCTIONS

1. Flour and salt in a basin.
2. In a large basin, using a hand or stand mixer on medium speed, cream the butter and sugar until creamy, about 2 to 3 minutes.

3. Stir in the egg, vanilla extract (and almond extract, if using), and almond extract until combined.

4. Slowly incorporate the flour into the mixture, stirring until a dough forms.

5. Place the dough in a basin and cover with plastic wrap. Refrigerate for a minimum of thirty minutes. Alternately, you can pipe out the dough first and then refrigerate the baking sheets!

6. To bake the cookies, preheat the oven to 350 degrees Fahrenheit and line two large baking sheets with parchment paper or a silicone baking mat.

7. Fit a pastry bag with the desired piping tip and fill it with the dough. When using a cookie press, adhere to the manufacturer's instructions.

8. Pipe the dough into 2-inch-long pieces, leaving about 1 inch between each section. Bake the cookies for 13 to 15 minutes, or until the edges are golden brown.

9. Cool the cookies for 5 minutes on the baking sheet before moving them to a cooling rack for final cooling.

10. Place the chocolate chips/chocolate in a microwave-safe bowl and microwave for 30 seconds, stirring the chocolate at each interval. Once the chocolate is approximately 75% melted, remove the bowl from the microwave and whisk the remaining chocolate. The remaining heat will perform all of the work!

11. Sprinkles, if used, should also be poured into a shallow bowl at this point.

12. Once the cookies have cooled, flip half of them over to form the bottom of the cookie sandwiches. Pipe or spoon 1/4 teaspoon of preserves on each bottom half, then sandwich with the top halves.

13. Dip the sandwiched cookies approximately one-third of the way into the melted chocolate, allowing the excess chocolate to drip off. Return the cookies to the baking sheet so that the chocolate may harden. You can also place them in the refrigerator for 5 to 10 minutes!

NOTES

Cookie dough may be frozen if desired; however, it must thaw overnight before baking. A week of cookie freshness can be maintained in an airtight container.

Italian Christmas Cookies

PREP TIME 20 mins

COOK TIME 45 mins

TOTAL TIME 1 hr 5 mins

SERVINGS 56

<u>INGREDIENTS</u>

For the Cookies:

- 6 big eggs
- 6 cups all-purpose flour
- 2 cups powdered sugar or confectioner's sugar
- 2½ teaspoons baking powder
- 1 cup shortening flavored with butter

- 1 tablespoon almond extract
- ½ tsp lemon extract

For the Glaze:

- 412 cups powdered sugar or confectioner's sugar
- 1/2 cup warm mild cream
- 1 teaspoon of almond extract
- 1 teaspoon vanilla extract
- colorful confetti

INSTRUCTIONS

1. Incorporate the eggs into a big bowl. Using a hand mixer on medium speed, beat the eggs on high speed for approximately 5 minutes, or until light and frothy.

2. Add five cups of flour, confectioners' sugar, and baking powder in a second large bowl. Whisk the ingredients to mix. Set aside.

3. Slowly incorporate the vegetable shortening and extracts while beating on low speed until the mixture resembles fine crumbs. Slowly include the beaten eggs.

4. Stir the flour mixture into one cup's egg mixture, thoroughly combining after each addition. The dough must be firm. If the dough is not stiff enough to roll into cookie balls, gradually add additional flour, beginning with a half cup. (Here is when the additional cup of flour comes into play) If the mixture is too loose, gently add the remaining half cup. At this point, the cookie dough should be firm enough to roll into balls.

5. Roll the dough into balls measuring 1 inch in diameter. Place cookies 2 inches apart on a parchment-lined baking sheet.

6. Bake at 350 degrees for 12 to 14 minutes. The cookies will not brown on top, but the bottoms should brown slightly.

7. To Cover The Cookies With Frosting

8. Thoroughly combine the confectioner's sugar, milk, and extracts in a small bowl.

9. Immediately after removing cookies from the oven, dip them twice or three times into the glaze.

10. Place on a wire rack with wax paper underneath to drain, then sprinkle immediately. Let dry 24 hours. To store, place in airtight containers.

Holy Cannoli Cookies

Prep Time15 minutes

Cook Time11 minutes

Total Time26 minutes

Yield36 cookies

Ingredients

- 1 cup unsalted butter softened
- 1 cup granulated sugar
- 2 big eggs
- 1/2 cup ricotta cheese
- 1 teaspoon vanilla extract
- 3/4 teaspoon cinnamon powder
- 1 teaspoon of fresh orange peel

- 1 teaspoon baking powder
- 1/2 teaspoon baking soda
- 1/2 teaspoon salt
- 2 cups all-purpose flour
- 10 ounces of miniature chocolate chips divided
- 1 cup finely chopped pistachios

Instructions

1. Using electric mixer, beat the butter and sugar in a large mixing basin until light and fluffy. Mix the eggs and ricotta cheese thoroughly before adding the vanilla extract, cinnamon, and orange zest.

2. Next, thoroughly combine the baking powder, baking soda, and salt. Blend in the flour. Incorporate the chocolate chips and pistachios. Chill dough for an hour.

3. Preheat oven 375 degrees F. Line baking sheets with parchment or gently oil them.

4. Using a small cookie scoop or spoon, drop approximately 1 1/2 tablespoons of cookie dough for each cookie, leaving approximately 2 inches of space between each biscuit.

5. Bake the cookies at 375 degrees Fahrenheit for 8 to 11 minutes, or until the edges are golden brown. Cool gently before transferring to wire racks for final cooling.

6. Microwave the remaining chocolate chips on high for 20 seconds in a small microwave-safe bowl, stirring until melted and smooth after each interval. Spoon melted chocolate into a tiny resealable bag, snip off one corner, and sprinkle chocolate over cookies. Allow chocolate to cool to solidify.

Notes

Tips: Some brands of chocolate chips melt better for dripping than others. A semisweet (or dark) chocolate bar will also work well in place of chocolate chips for melting and drizzling. After baking, these cookies do not need to be refrigerated. Similar to other cookies, store these in an airtight bag or container.

ITALIAN CHRISTMAS COOKIES

Prep Time: 15 minutes

Cook Time: 13 minutes

Total Time: 28 minutes

Servings: 35 cookies

Ingredients

- 3/4 cup of room-temperature unsalted butter (1 1/2 sticks)
- 1⅓ cup granulated sugar
- 4 big eggs
- 3 tsp vanilla extract
- 1 tsp almond extract (maybe be substituted with lemon, zest, or juice).
- 3¾ cup all-purpose flour
- 1 tablespoon cornflour
- 4 tsp baking powder
- ½ tsp salt Glaze
- 2 cups confectioners' sugar powder
- 2 tablespoons cold water
- 2 tsp almond extract
- Christmas sprinkles or jimmies

Instructions

1. Whisk flour, cornstarch, baking powder, and salt in a bowl.

2. In a bowl fitted with a mixer, whip butter and sugar high for approximately 5 minutes until light and fluffy.

3. Add eggs one mixing until integrated after each addition. Add vanilla and almond extracts to a mixer.

4. Slowly incorporate dry ingredients into wet ingredients. Beat until thoroughly mixed.

5. Cover the bowl and refrigerate for a minimum of four hours or overnight.

6. Preheating the oven to 350°F. Grease or line baking pans with parchment paper.

7. The dough is sticky. You may use a cookie scoop or a tablespoon to scoop dough onto baking sheets. TIP: If the scoop becomes sticky, dunk it between scoops in a bowl of powdered sugar. Separate cookies by 1 inch.

8. Bake in the oven for 13 to 15 minutes, or until the sides are golden brown.

9. Permit to cool. Move the dish to a cooling rack.

10. If desired, pat the tops of the cookies with a flat spatula after baking to reduce the puffiness. This makes frosting and sprinkling easier.

11. Combine powdered sugar, water, and almond essence in a medium bowl. Blend until smooth.

12. Apply glaze to each cookie with a spoon over a cookie rack, with sprinkles on top.

AMARETTO TRICOLOR COOKIES

Ingredients

Almond Paste

- 1.5 cups almond meal
- 1 cup sifted powdered sugar
- 1/2 tsp almond extract
- 2 Tbsp water

Cookie Layers

- 4 1/4 ounces (1 cup) of all-purpose flour
- 1/4 tsp salt
- 7 ounces of almond paste (by weight)
- 3/4 cup granulated sugar
- 1/2 tsp almond extract
- 3/4 tablespoons (1 1/2 sticks) cubed unsalted butter
- 3 big eggs
- One orange zest (I used a tangelo)
- Orange gel food coloring (or your preferred color) sufficient to create a bright layer
- 2 tablespoons of unsweetened dark cocoa

Filling

- 2/3 cup apricot jam
- 2 tbsp Amaretto liquor Chocolate Glaze
- 6 ounces of dark chocolate (60 percent cacao)

- 1 tsp corn syrup, mild
- 1/2 cup (1 stick) cubed unsalted butter, unsalted

Instructions

Almond Spread

1. Place all ingredients in a food processor and pulse until a paste forms.
2. Cover with plastic wrap and chill until required.
3. Cookie Dough or Cookie Batter
4. Preheating the oven to 350 degrees F.
5. Butter three eight-inch square cake pans, then line the bottoms with parchment paper and butter the paper. Using two pans, bake layers separately.
6. Flour and salt are whisked together.
7. Mix almond paste, sugar, and almond extract in a stand mixer with the paddle attachment.
8. High-speed mixer, butter. Add the eggs one by one until well integrated.
9. Add the zest and stir to incorporate.
10. Add the flour mixture in thirds, mixing on low until barely incorporated after each addition.
11. Distribute the batter among three bowls (I weighed the dough to ensure each layer had an equal amount). Add cocoa to one, orange food coloring to another, and leave one uncolored.
12. Spread the dough/batter evenly in each cake pan, creating an even layer.
13. Bake for approximately 12 to 15 minutes.

14.   Allow layers to cool 20 minutes in the pans before turning them onto a wire rack. Take away the parchment.

Filling

1. Combine the jam and Amaretto in a saucepan and cook for 3 to 5 minutes. If your jam is too lumpy, use a hand blender to smooth it out.
2. Allow cooling for a few minutes before use.
3. Chocolate Glaze
4. Combine the chocolate, corn syrup, and butter in a double boiler or a stainless steel bowl set over simmering water.
5. Constantly stir until smooth.

Assembly

1. Place the chocolate layer in a jelly roll or quarter sheet pan coated with parchment paper. Spread half of the filling on it.
2. Place the white layer above the chocolate layer and spread the remaining filling on top.
3. Place the orange layer on top and use your hands to push the layers together gently.
4. Place the layers in the refrigerator for at least five minutes while preparing the chocolate glaze.
5. Spread the glaze throughout the layers.
6. Refrigerate for a minimum of one hour.
7. Bring the dish to room temperature for 30 minutes.
8. Transfer the parchment to a cutting board and slice the layers into bars. I cut my cookies into one-inch squares, yielding 36 cookies.
9. Refrigerate in an airtight jar for up to four days.

Italian Lemon Cookies

YIELD: 4-5 DOZEN

COOK TIME10 minutes

TOTAL TIME10 minutes

Ingredients

For the Cookies:

- 3 eggs
- 1/2 cup milk
- 3-5 drops lemon oil or 2 tablespoons lemon extract
- 1/2 cup oil
- 3 cups all-purpose flour
- 8 tablespoons of baking powder
- 1/2 cup sugar

For the Ice Cream:

- 6 cups confectioners' sugar
- a half-cup of milk (or more as needed)
- 2-3 drops of lemon oil

Instructions

For the Cookie Recipe:

1. Preheat oven to 350 degrees Celsius.
2. Prepare cookie sheets by coating them lightly with shortening. Set aside.
3. Thoroughly incorporate the eggs, milk, lemon oil, sugar, and vegetable oil in the stand mixer bowl.
4. Add the flour and baking powder, 1 cup and a few teaspoons at a time, to the mixture.

5. Mix until a dough is formed. It will be quite tacky. To make the dough workable, add flour.

6. Using a cookie scoop dunked in flour, drop the cookies onto the prepared baking sheets, leaving approximately an inch between each cookie.

7. Bake until the tops are softly golden brown.

8. Transfer the cookies directly from the baking pan to a cooling rack.

9. Permit the cookies to cool before icing completely.

To Prepare the Icing:

1. Combine powdered sugar, milk, and lemon oil or essence in a large bowl.

2. add more milk to achieve the appropriate consistency. The frosting should be thick but runny.

3. Place the wax paper beneath the cookies on the wire rack.

4. Employing a spoon, drizzle the icing over the cookies.

5. Add sprinkles if desired.

BEFANINI

Prep Time50 mins

Cook Time15 mins

Total Time1 hr 5 mins

Servings: 50 cookies

Ingredients

- 4 cups flour

- 14 tablespoons unsalted butter, soft

- 1 cup sugar

- ¼ cup milk

- Lemon zest of one

- 5 eggs

- ½ teaspoon baking powder

- 1 teaspoon of salt

- 2 tablespoons rum

- Small multicolored sprinkles

Instructions

1. Eggs and sugar are whisked until frothy.

2. Combine the butter, flour, milk, baking powder, salt, lemon zest, and rum in a bowl (optional).

3. Mix ingredients into a dough.

4. Allow sitting in the refrigerator for 45 minutes.

5. Preheating the oven to 350F/180C.

6. Spread the dough with a rolling pin to a thickness of about 18 inches (4 mm) Create shapes with cookie cutters.

7. Brush the cookies with egg yolk and place them on a baking sheet that has been buttered, floured, or lined with parchment paper.

8. Sprinkle with sugar sprinkles.

9. Bake for approximately 15 minutes.

10. Observe the color of the betanin, as they should not be too dark.

Italian Christmas Cookies

prep time: 50 MINUTES

Ingredients

- 3/4 cup softened butter
- 1/2 cup confectioners' sugar
- 1/2 cup sugar
- 3 eggs
- 3 cups flour
- 3 tablespoons baking powder
- 1/2 teaspoon salt
- 1 teaspoon vanilla
- 1/2 teaspoon anise extract
- Extra powder sugar

Glaze

- 2 cups confectioners' sugar
- 3 tablespoons milk
- 1 teaspoon vanilla extract
- Nonpareil Sprinkles

Instructions

1. Whisk flour, salt, and baking powder in a medium bowl. Set aside.
2. In a mixing dish, blend butter and sugars.
3. Add the eggs one by one. Then, flavor with vanilla and anise.
4. Mix in the flour mixture gradually. Do not overbeat the drums.
5. Refrigerate dough for 60 minutes.

6. Preheat the oven to 350 degrees before baking. Line a sheet pan with parchment paper.

7. Roll the dough into one-inch balls. Use the bottom of a tiny glass dipped in powdered sugar to press each ball down.

8. Bake for 8-10 minutes.

9. Remove and allow to cool completely.

To make the glaze:

1. In a bowl, sift two cups of powdered sugar. Whisk in milk and vanilla.

2. Dip each cookie's top into the glaze. Decorate with nonpareil sprinkles.

3. Allow the glaze to dry before freezing.

Double Chocolate Biscotti

Prep Time:10 minutes

Cook Time:50 minutes

Resting Time:5 minutes

Total Time:1 hour 5 minutes

Ingredients

CUPSMETRIC

- 6 teaspoons vegan butter
- ¾ cup granulated sugar
- 2 tablespoons flaxseed meal
- 2 teaspoons cornstarch
- a half-cup of plant-based milk
- one-fourth teaspoon almond extract
- 2 cups all-purpose flour
- one and one-half tablespoons of baking powder
- ¼ cup cocoa powder

- 1/2 cup non-dairy chocolate chips

CHOCOLATE TOPPING

- 3/4 cup non-dairy chocolate chips
- 1 teaspoon coconut oil

BISCOTTI INSTRUCTIONS:

1. preheat oven 350 degrees F Line a baking sheet with parchment paper to prepare it for use.

2. Place the butter in a bowl for mixing. Use a handheld or stand mixer on medium speed to whip the ingredients until frothy. Add sugar and continue beating until light and airy. Add flax, cornstarch, milk, and extract to the mixture. Again, beat to combine.

3. Add the flour, baking powder, and cocoa powder to the bowl and blend at a low pace. Incorporate the chocolate chips.

4. Transfer the dough to the baking dish that has been prepared. The dough is divided in half and patted into two logs measuring roughly 9.5 inches. Each loaf must be about three-quarters of an inch tall. Sprinkle coarse sugar on top.

5. Bake between 20 and 25 minutes. Then, remove the biscotti loaves from the oven and allow them to cool for approximately 10 minutes.

6. Spray both loaves with water at room temperature using a spray bottle.

7. Reduce oven temperature to 300°F/150°C and set loaves on a cutting board. Using a serrated knife, cut loaves into roughly 34-inch thick slices. Return these slices to the pans and bake them for 10 minutes. Remove the slices from the oven, flip them over, and bake for an additional 10 minutes.

8. Place the biscotti on a wire rack to cool completely after baking.

FOR THE CANDIED TOPPING:

1. In a microwave-safe bowl, mix the chocolate chips and coconut oil. Microwave the chocolate in 30-second increments until it has melted. Stir to mix.

2. Dip the bottom of each cookie into the melted chocolate and place it waxed or parchment paper.

3. Drizzle additional melted chocolate mixture on top of each cookie. Set cookies aside until the chocolate has hardened, or transfer the pan to the refrigerator to hasten the process.

4. Once the chocolate has solidified, store the cookies airtight. They will last up to 10 days at room temperature and 20 days in the refrigerator. In freezer-safe containers or bags, they can be frozen for three months.

Notes

TO DIPPING OR NOT TO DIPPING

- You do not have to dip the cookies in chocolate if you do not wish to. However, it is a very charming touch, particularly when they are being given as gifts.

CUTTING LOAVES

- When slicing biscotti loaves, you can either turn them on their sides and cut the cookies diagonally or arrange the loaf with the long end facing away from you and make horizontal slices down the loaf. Both approaches are viable.

Classic Easy Panettone Cake Recipe

Prep Time30 mins

Cook Time50 mins

Rising time3 hrs

Total Time4 hrs 20 mins

Servings: 1 cake

Ingredients

- 4 tablespoons warm milk
- 1 tablespoon dry yeast
- 8 tbsp sugar
- 2 sticks of room-temperature butter
- 5 big eggs beaten
- 2 tsp vanilla extract
- zest of 1 lemon, grated
- 1 orange zest grated
- 2 1/4 cups flour
- salt to taste
- 7 tbsp raisins
- 3 tbsp rum extract
- 8 tbsp chopped candied lemon and orange peel
- butter for greasing

For the topping

- 1 tablespoon egg white
- 1 tbsp icing sugar
- add extra powdered sugar for dusting

Equipment

- Panettone cake pan
- big mixing bowl

- silicone brush
- big spoon
- hand mixer
- tiny saucepan

Instructions

1. Grease a pan for Panettone with melted butter.
2. Pour the warm milk into a bowl, add the yeast and 1 tsp of sugar, and stir well.
3. Combine the remaining sugar, butter, and vanilla extract in a large bowl and beat with a hand mixer until light and fluffy.
4. Mix in lemon and orange zest.
5. Add eggs one by one until blended.
6. If the mixture curdles, whisk in 1 tablespoon flour.
7. Form a well in the flour and salt.
8. Add yeast mixture, followed by the butter and egg combination, and incorporate with a large spoon to create a soft dough.
9. Knead the mixture in the bowl for five minutes, or until it begins to come together and is somewhat sticky.
10. Knead the dough for until it is soft and malleable. Add a tiny dusting of flour to the surface and your hands to prevent the mixture from sticking while you work.
11. Place in a lightly greased basin and cover with plastic wrap; let rise in a warm location for two hours, or until it has doubled in size.
12. Place the raisins and rum essence in a small saucepan over low heat for about 5 minutes, or until the fruit has absorbed the liquor; leave aside to cool.

13.   When the dough has risen, turn it out onto a lightly floured area and knead it for a further five minutes. Mix in the soaked raisins and chopped candied peel gradually. Form the dough into a ball and place it in the Panettone pan. Using thread, tie a layer of baking parchment around the outside of an 8-inch deep cake pan to extend approximately 2 inches above the rim. This will help contain the rising dough.

14.   Cover and let rise for until dough reaches pan or parchment paper.

15.   Preheat the oven to 350 °F.

16.   Combine the confectioner's sugar and egg white and brush the mixture over the top of the Panettone.

17.   Place the Panettone in oven and bake for 40 to 50 minutes, or until golden brown and puffed. Check the cake's doneness with a skewer.

18.   Allow for 10 minutes in the pan before transferring to a cooling rack.

19.   Cool before powdering with sugar.

20.   Serve cut into wedges.

Mini Chocolate Panettone

Servings: 6 mini panettones

Prep Time: 30 mins

Cook Time: 25 mins

Ingredients

- 1/3 cup tepid milk (80 ml)

- ½ teaspoon sugar
- 2 1/4 tablespoons dry yeast
- 2 cups bread flour (260 gr)
- 1 teaspoon salt
- half a lemon zest
- the rind of one orange
- 1 ½ teaspoon vanilla extract
- 1 egg, room temperature
- 1 egg yolk served at room temperature
- 1 spoonful of honey (40 gr)
- 1/3 cup butter (75 grams), diced and at room temperature
- 5-ounce chocolate chip (100 gr)
- 1 egg mixed with a splash of milk, egg wash

Instructions

1. Combine sugar and milk, then add dry yeast. Combine and allow the yeast to activate.
2. Pour the remaining ingredients into an upright mixing bowl, except the chocolate chips, butter, and egg wash. Add yeast mixture as well. 10 minutes of kneading after a thorough blending.
3. Add the butter in increments, incorporating it thoroughly after each addition. Once all of the butter has been included, knead for a further 10 minutes. Place dough in a greased bowl, cover with cling film, and allow to rise until it doubles in size.
4. Lightly lubricate your work surface. We don't want to incorporate more flour into the dough, so refrain from using flour. The dough is placed and lightly pressed into a square shape.

5. Sprinkle chocolate chips on top and knead the dough briefly to distribute the chocolate chunks evenly. Roll each dough half into a ball. Place the balls in the small panettone cases (2.5 by 1.75 inches or 6.35 by 4.4 centimeters) on a baking sheet. This will facilitate the subsequent transfer into the oven.

6. Cover and let dough rise until complete. Apply an egg wash to the surface with a brush. Bake at 350°F (175°C) for 25 minutes. Enjoy!

Authentic Italian Tiramisu Recipe

Servings: 12 servings

Prep20 minutes

Chill8 hours

Total8 hours 20 minutes

Ingredients

- 3 big egg yolks, cool
- 1 cup sifted, unpackaged powdered sugar
- 2 ¼ cups full-fat mascarpone, cold
- 27-36 Italian ladyfingers (hard ones)
- one-half cup of cold espresso or strong coffee
- 2 teaspoon chocolate powder, unsweetened

Instructions

1. In a bowl fitted with a whisk attachment, beat the egg yolks and powdered sugar until smooth and dissolved.

2. Add the mascarpone and mix at medium speed until smooth and creamy, approximately one minute.

3. Place 9 to 12 ladyfingers on the bottom of a 9 x 7 x 3–inch (23 x 18 x 8 cm) or an 8 x 8 x 3–inch (20 x 20 cm) casserole dish. The number of ladyfingers required will depend on the size of the ladyfingers and the casserole dish. The amount of coffee necessary depends on how long the ladyfingers are dipped and how much they absorb. The resulting tiramisu will be quite watery if you soak the ladyfingers for too long.

4. Spread approximately one-third of the mascarpone cream over the ladyfingers. Repeat twice more so that the Tiramisu is formed as follows: ladyfingers and cream, ladyfingers and cream, ladyfingers and cream, and ladyfingers and cream.

5. Cover the casserole dish securely with plastic wrap to prevent air and aromas from the refrigerator from entering the tiramisu. Refrigerate for 8-12 hours overnight. Before serving, lightly coat the surface with cocoa powder. Refrigerate for up to three days.

Notes Advice

1. Use a large mixing bowl to combine the mascarpone ingredients. This reduces the likelihood of overmixing the mascarpone.

2. I recommend just using fresh eggs. If an egg does not appear or smell fresh, do not consume it.

3. Do not skip the chilling period. Tiramisu is finest the second day after preparation. The flavor improves when allowed to rest in the refrigerator overnight, and the consistency becomes creamier.

Eggs

It is safe to ingest pasteurized eggs raw because they have been cooked within their shells. They're hard to find and poorly distributed.

Before adding the egg yolks and sugar to the mascarpone, you can also boil them. Mix the mascarpone with an electric mixer on medium speed until it is smooth and creamy, then put aside. For cooking the egg yolks and sugar, a double boiler is required. Set a heat-safe bowl on a saucepan containing 2 inches (5 cm) of simmering water if you do not have a double boiler. Continuously whisk the egg yolks and sugar for about 5 minutes, or until bubbly and fluffy. Then, remove from heat and combine with mascarpone cheese until smooth and creamy.

If you don't want to use any eggs, stir the mascarpone cheese for around one to two minutes until it becomes creamy. Then, incorporate the powdered sugar for two to three minutes, or until the sugar is dissolved and the mixture is smooth. Consider that without the egg yolks, there is less cream. In this instance, I suggest constructing a two-layer tiramisu or whisking 12 cups (120ml) of heavy cream into the mascarpone mixture until firm peaks form.

Dark Rum

You might add two tablespoons (30 milliliters) of rum to the coffee where the ladyfingers are dipped. Additionally, 1 tablespoon of rum can be added to the mascarpone cream. Additionally, you might use Amaretto or brandy.

Frothy Cream

If you want to add heavy whipping cream to your mascarpone cream, add 12 cups (120ml) of heavy whipping cream and mix on medium-high speed for about 2 minutes, or until stiff peaks form.

You may add whipped cream to the chilled tiramisu before dusting it with chocolate. Simply pipe small dollops of whipped cream on top to reproduce the picture-perfect top. I utilized a circular Wilton 1A tip with my piping bag.

Gluten-Free

This dish can be made gluten-free by substituting gluten-free ladyfingers for conventional ones.

Coffee

If you wish to offer this dessert to children or caffeine-sensitive individuals, you may substitute decaffeinated coffee or hot cocoa.

Italian Chocolate Toto Cookies

Prep Time: 20 minutes

Cook Time: 20 minutes

Total Time: 40 minutes

Servings: 48

Ingredients

- 3 ¼ cups 406.25 grams of All-Purpose flour
- 1 ½ cup 300 grams of sugar
- 1 Tablespoon baking powder
- ¼ cup 21.5 grams of natural cocoa
- 1 12 tablespoons freshly ground, not too coarsely powdered black pepper
- 1 1/4 tablespoons clove powder

- 1 1/2 tablespoons cinnamon powder
- ½ teaspoon salt
- ¾ cup 153.75 grams solid vegetable shortening
- ½ to ⅔ cup 122-162 ⅔ grams of milk
- 1 teaspoon Fiori di Sicilia Orange and Vanilla flavor
- 78 grams (2/3 cup) chopped walnuts
- 1 cup or 175 grams of mini-chocolate chips (6 oz.)

GLAZE:

- 1 1/2 cups or 180 grams of sifted confectioner's sugar
- 1 Tablespoonful of Cocoa
- 3 to 3 ½ Tablespoons milk
- colored sprinkles for adornment
- 1 teaspoon Fiori di Sicilia flavoring orange and vanilla flavor

Instructions

1. Preheat oven 350 degrees F (180 C). Spray parchment paper with cooking spray and set it on cookie sheets.
2. On wax paper, sift dry ingredients. I repeated this process four times to thoroughly blend the ingredients.
3. Put the dry ingredients into the food processor's bowl. Add the emulsifier. Repeatedly pulse the mixture in a food processor until it resembles a coarse meal. This can be done manually, but it is quick and simple using a processor.
4. Mix the Fiori di Sicilia with a half cup of milk.
5. Pour the combination of dry ingredients into a large bowl. Stir in the chopped nuts and chocolate chips to mix them.

6. Add milk to the dry ingredients and incorporate it with your hands until everything is thoroughly combined. If the dough seems dry, add milk until it's cohesive but not sticky.

7. Knead the dough on a non-stick Silpat or a wooden board. Then, divide into four equal pieces. Twist each piece into a rope. Cut the rope into twelve equal pieces. Form each piece into a ball and place it on the parchment paper.

8. Place on the paper 1 inch apart. Proceed with each rope.

9. Bake for until they have reached a hard consistency.

10. While the cookies cool, prepare the glaze.

11. Repeatedly sift the confectioner's sugar and cocoa until thoroughly mixed. Combine the mixture, 3 tablespoons of milk, and seasoning in a bowl. Beat until creamy. If required, add additional milk to create a thin frosting.

12. Once the cookies have cooled, dip the tops in the icing, lay them on wax paper-lined racks, and sprinkle them with the colorful sprinkles.

13. Allow the icing to dry thoroughly before stacking the cookies between wax or parchment paper. They can be stored for up to one week in an airtight container or frozen for two months.

Tiramisu Semifreddo Recipe

Prep Time20 mins

Total Time20 mins

Servings: 6 people

Ingredients

- ½ cup (4oz/115g) mascarpone cheese
- 1 cup (8 oz/225 ml) of heavy cream
- 1/2 cup (5 ounce/142 grams) cold sweetened condensed milk
- Dilute 2 teaspoons of instant coffee granules with 4 tablespoons of water
- 3/4 cup (6 ounces/170 milliliters) of robustly brewed coffee
- optional 1/4 cup (2 oz/57 ml) brandy
- 12 ladyfingers, about

Instructions

1. Grease and line a 9-by-5-inch loaf pan with three pieces of plastic wrap. This will allow you to remove the semifreddo from the tin later.
2. Whip the mascarpone cheese on medium-high speed using a stand mixer or an electric hand mixer.
3. Pour the cream into the mixture and continue beating until soft peaks form.
4. Reduce the mixer's speed slightly and add the cold condensed milk and diluted coffee to the whipped cream mixture.
5. Then, increase the machine's speed to high and whisk the mixture until it is thick and forms firm peaks.
6. Pour approximately one-third of the cream mixture into the loaf pan and spread to cover the bottom of the pan.
7. In a shallow dish, combine the strong-brewed coffee and brandy.
8. Quickly soak each ladyfinger in the coffee and set them in the loaf pan. Resist the temptation to dunk longer; they only require a few seconds in the coffee mixture.

9. After layering ladyfingers, spoon another one-third of the cream mixture on top and continue layering ladyfingers. After two layers, smooth the remaining cream mixture over the top. I enjoy striking it against the counter to level it.

10.   Before eating, freeze for at least 5 hours or overnight. Serve the cake on a cocoa-dusted dish. The semifreddo can be kept in the freezer for up to six weeks.

Pizzelle Della Nonna

Prep Time: 10 minutes

Cook Time: 1 hour

Total Time: 1 hour 10 minutes

Servings: 30 servings

Ingredients

- 1¼ cups all-purpose flour 177 grams
- 3/4 teaspoon baking powder
- pinch salt
- 3 eggs at room temperature
- ½ cup sugar 100 grams
- ¼ cup vegetable oil
- 1 teaspoon vanilla extract
- 1 teaspoon optional anise extract

Instructions

1. Preheat pizzelle iron.
2. Sift together flour, baking powder, and salt in a medium bowl. Set aside.

3. In a large mixing bowl or the bowl of an electric mixer fitted with the whisk attachment, beat the eggs until foamy and the mixture begins to thicken (about 2-3 minutes).

4. Add sugar. Continue whisking until the mixture is sufficiently thickened, approximately 3 to 4 minutes.

5. Add the vegetable oil and extracts. Mix thoroughly.

6. Slowly include the flour mixture at a low speed until the dough is moist and sticky.

7. Pour one spoonful of batter into a heated pizzelle press. Additionally, you can use a small cookie scoop.

8. Cook for 30 to 45 seconds until browned.

9. Using a fork, remove the food from the press.

10.   Transfer the mixture to a flat surface or form it into the desired shape.

11.   Scroll UP for PHOTOS OF EACH STEP

12.   Don't miss the process photos and videos featured in most entries. Just scroll up the post to locate them. These were designed specifically for you to execute the recipe properly every time.

Notes

- The required specialized equipment for this dish is a pizzelle iron.
- To create chocolate pizzelle, sift together 1 cup of all-purpose flour (142 grams), and 14 cups unsweetened cocoa powder (21 grams). Leave out the anise extract.
- Can they be made vegan? Yes. These are the modifications you must make. Replace the eggs with 3 tsp of ground flaxseed and 9 tablespoons

of water at room temperature. 14 cups + 1 tablespoon of oil is required. Also, ensure that the sugar you are using has not been treated with bone char.

- Please note that the nutritional information provided below is an approximation and that differences may occur based on the ingredients utilized.

Cannolis

PREP TIME15 mins

INACTIVE TIME12 hrs

TOTAL TIME12 hrs 15 mins

SERVINGS8 cannolis

Ingredients

- Eight cannoli shells, homemade or purchased, will suffice
- 2 cups ricotta cheese
- 1 cup confectioner's sugar plus additional sugar for dusting
- 3/4 cup small chocolate chips, split
- tablespoons of pure vanilla extract

Optional:

- 2 tablespoons freshly grated orange peel

Instructions

2. Place ricotta cheese in a strainer with a fine mesh and place it in the refrigerator for at least 12 hours and up to 24 hours to drain.
3. When ready to prepare the filling:

4. Combine the drained ricotta cheese, confectioners' sugar, 14 cups of the mini chocolate chips, vanilla essence, and orange zest in a large bowl; stir thoroughly. Carefully scrape the mixture into a pastry bag with a 1/2-inch open tip using a spatula. Use immediately or refrigerate until required; the filling can be prepared up to 24 hours beforehand.

5. When ready to serve, pipe the filling into one end of the cannoli shell, then into the other end. If you do not have a pastry bag, you may place the filling in the shells with a spoon. Continue with the remaining shells.

6. Place the remainder of the little chocolate chips on a small platter. Coat each end of the cannoli with chocolate chips, then sprinkle with confectioners' sugar. Serve immediately

NOTES

The filling can be prepared and refrigerated for up to 24 hours. Once the cannoli shells have been filled, they should be served immediately. Cannolis should be consumed the same day they are produced.

Pandoro Christmas Tree Cake

Prep Time15 minutes

Total Time15 minutes

Servings12 people

Ingredients

- 1 large Pandoro cake
- 2 cups Mascarpone (17.5 oz/500g)
- 1 fl ounce Vin Santo or liquor of choice (30ml)
- 1/2 cup confectioners' sugar plus 1 tsp for dusting (70g)

- ¼ cup pistachios plus a few extra to decorate (25g)
- 1/2 cup finely chopped white chocolate (50g)
- 1/2 cup Red currants or pomegranate, plus additional for garnish (3.5 oz/100g)

Instructions

1. Whisk together the mascarpone, vin santo, and powdered sugar in a large mixing basin for one minute. Stir in the white chocolate and pistachios before setting them away.
2. Cut the pandoro into five pieces from the bottom up. Spread the mascarpone mixture evenly on each layer, scattering a few red currents on each layer.
3. As you layer the mascarpone mixture, stack the pandoro slices like a Christmas tree, with the points not matching.
4. Garnish with powdered sugar and additional red currents and pistachios.

Notes

- Utilize a serrated bread knife to section the cake.
- Pistachios give the cake a festive green hue, but you may substitute other nuts.
- You can also use milk or dark chocolate for the white chocolate.
- When freezing the leftover cake, cover it tightly in plastic wrap and aluminum foil.
- You can follow this recipe with panettone (it will be wonderful), but you won't achieve the same Christmas tree appearance.
- Red currants can be substituted with pomegranate.

Easy Struffoli Recipe

Prep Time: 10 minutes

Cook Time: 25 minutes

Total Time: 35 minutes

Servings: 10 servings

Ingredients

- 1 cup flour
- 1 lemon zest
- 1 orange zest
- 1.5 tbsp sugar
- 1/4 tsp salt
- 1/4 tsp baking powder
- 2 ounces of unsalted butter
- 2 eggs medium
- 1/3 tsp vanilla extract
- 1/2 teaspoon of rum or brandy
- For frying, use vegetable or canola oil.
- one-half cup honey
- 1/4 cup sugar
- 1/2 tbsp lemon juice
- sprinkles
- "sweetened fruits."
- Sugar for confections

Instructions

Blending the dough

1. Mix the flour, citrus zest, sugar, salt, and baking powder.
2. Butter and dry ingredients in a food processor. Blend until practically all-butter lumps have disappeared. Mixture should be grainy.

3. Add the eggs and vanilla essence slowly. Combine the ingredients until the dough resembles a large ball.

4. Cover the dough with plastic wrap and refrigerate for at least thirty minutes.

5. Next, roll the dough into cords approximately a quarter of an inch thick. Cut the dough into approximately half-inch parts and roll each portion into a small ball. Each ball of dough should be roughly the size of a standard hazelnut.

6. Dust the dough balls lightly with flour. Ensure that everyone is covered, but don't add too much flour.

7. Sauté the dough balls.

8. Place some oil in a saucepan over medium heat. Using a thermometer, monitor the current temperature. Bring to 375°F.

9. Fry the balls of dough in batches. Each batch should take approximately two to three minutes. The color of dough balls should have a golden hue.

10. Line a serving platter with paper towels in the interim.

11. Place the finished dough balls on the plate and allow the paper towels to absorb the excess oil.

12. Coating the dough balls with glaze

13. Combine honey, lemon juice, rum (or brandy), and sugar in a saucepan. Prepare the mixture over medium heat.

14. Stir the honey mixture continuously with a spatula, and simmer until the sugar is completely dissolved.

15. Carefully add the fried dough balls to the mixture once it's ready. Carefully combine the ingredients so as not to harm the dough.

16.   Once all dough balls have been coated with the honey mixture, move them to a serving dish. Reserve the leftover mixture.

17.   Place the dough balls around the edge of the serving tray, leaving a hole in the center. You can set a glass in the center to estimate the size of the hole you are producing. You can also create a mound of dough balls in the center for a simpler assembling.

18.   After placing the dough balls on the serving platter, drizzle the remaining honey mixture on top with care. Include as much as you desire.

19.   Next, immediately cover the dough balls with sprinkles, confectioner's sugar, or edible decorations.

20.   Serve without delay!

PANNA COTTA

YIELD: 4 servings

Ingredients

- 1/4 cup (60 ml) chilled milk or water
- 2 1/4 teaspoons (7 grams/0.25 ounces) unflavored gelatin powder
- 2 cups (480 milliliters) heavy cream
- 1/4 cup (50 g/1.8 oz.) granulated sugar
- One-half vanilla bean, split and seeded, or one teaspoon vanilla extract

Instructions

1. Pour water into a small bowl and evenly sprinkle gelatin over the surface. Not stacking it will prevent the crystals from dissolving effectively. Allow sitting for 5 to 10 minutes to soften.

2. In the meantime, bring cream, sugar, vanilla bean, and vanilla seeds to a boil in a saucepan over medium heat until the sugar has dissolved. Remove from heat and throw away the vanilla bean. Add gelatin, then whisk immediately until smooth and dissolved. If the gelatin has not completely dissolved, return the pot to the burner over low heat. Continuously stir and do not allow the mixture to boil.

3. Pour cream into four separate serving bowls. Refrigerate for at least two to four hours, or until set.

4. If desired, add fresh fruit, berries, berry sauce, or lemon curd.

5. Cover panna cotta with plastic wrap and chill for up to three days.

Christmas Ice Cream Cake

Prep Time15 minutes

freezing time8 hours

Total Time8 hours 15 minutes

Servings10 servings

Ingredients

- 1 Panettone (26 oz/750g)
- Semifreddo ingredients
- 1 cup heavy cream double cream (250ml)
- 1 cup of condensed milk (394g)
- ¼ cup sugar (50g)
- 1 teaspoon vanilla extract
- 1 fl oz Cointreau (30ml/1 part)

Topping

- 1 cup dark chocolate (200g)
- sprinkles, for decorating

Instructions

1. Remove the panettone's paper wrapping, including the bottom, and slice it into 1/2-inch-thick slices.

2. Lining a bowl with plastic wrap (cling film) leaves enough overlap for cake wrapping. Place one slice of panettone at the bottom of the bowl and lightly press it down.

3. Continue adding panettone slices around the sides of the bowl, making sure they overlap, so there are no gaps, then press the cake down and set it aside.

4. Next, combine all semifreddo ingredients in a stand mixer until soft peaks form. Be careful not to overmix the ingredients.

5. Pour the ice cream or semifreddo mixture into the panettone-lined bowl and carefully tuck in any overhanging panettone.

6. Add another slice (or more if necessary) to cover the ice cream mixture's surface.

7. Fold over the overlapped plastic wrap to cover the cake's surface thoroughly, then freeze.

8. When the Christmas ice cream cake is ready to be served, melt dark chocolate in a basin over simmering water.

9. Place the panettone bombe on a wire rack placed over a baking sheet, pour the melted chocolate over the top and sprinkle with festive sprinkles.

10. Within a minute or two, the chocolate will solidify and be ready to serve.

Notes

- The panettone bombe should be cuttable after 5 to 10 minutes out of the freezer.
- I like dark chocolate because the panettone and ice cream are extremely sweet, but feel free to use milk or even white chocolate.
- Feel free to substitute Cointreau with your preferred liquor or omit it entirely.
- Ensure that the bowl and plastic wrap (cling film) are freezer-safe.
- You can use any sprinkles you desire, and edible glitter is usually a wonderful addition.

HOMEMADE TORRONE ITALIAN NUT NOUGAT

PREP TIME: 15 MINUTES

COOK TIME: 1 HOUR 30 MINUTES

COOL: 3 HOURS

TOTAL TIME: 4 HOURS 45 MINUTES

SERVINGS: 12

INGREDIENTS

- Two sheets of wafer paper trimmed to suit an 8x8-inch pan
- 12 ounces of honey
- 1 2/3 cup white sugar
- three egg whites served at room temperature
- 1 Dash salt
- 1 teaspoon of clear vanilla extract for a whiter torrone

- 1 Tablespoon lemon zest
- toasted almonds, pistachios, hazelnuts, or pecans, 3 cups

<u>INSTRUCTIONS</u>

1. Prepare a 9-inch square baking dish (or one similar size) by covering the bottom and sides with plastic wrap. Cut both wafer paper sheets to the dimensions of your baking dish. Place one sheet of wafer paper in the dish's bottom and keep aside the second sheet for later use.

2. Beat the egg whites with a pinch of salt in a stand mixer until soft peaks form. Keep the ingredients in the stand mixer.

3. Place the honey and sugar in a medium to a big pot with a heavy bottom. Stir this mixture until it reaches 300 degrees Fahrenheit over medium heat.

4. Once the sugar mixture reaches 300 degrees, remove it from the heat and transfer it immediately to a stand mixer. Stream approximately 3 tablespoons of the hot sugar mixture into the egg whites while the mixer is on medium-high speed. Allow the sugar mixture to blend with the egg whites and beat for a few moments before slowly incorporating the remaining sugar mixture.

5. Add lemon zest and vanilla extract to the mixture. Pay close watch to how thick the mixture becomes as it cools, and continue to whip it until the sides of the bowl are cool enough to hold your hand on for 10 seconds. Add the nuts, give it a thorough stir, and then turn off the mixer when this occurs. Nonetheless, if the mixture becomes too thick before the bowl is cool enough to handle, add the nuts and stop mixing at any time.

6. Quickly spoon the batter on the wafer paper into the prepared baking dish. Spread as evenly as possible with care. You may use a lightly oiled spatula to spread the nougat if necessary.

7. Place the second wafer paper sheet atop the nougat. Use the bottom of a cup or ramekin to help smooth out the surface.

8. Allow cooling to room temperature.

9. When ready, transfer the torrone to a cutting board with caution. Remove the plastic wrap and cut the torrone into the proper sizes using a long, serrated knife.

Mostaccioli di Mamma

Prep Time: 1 hour

Cook Time: 20 minutes

Total Time: 1 hour 20 minutes

Servings: 60

Ingredients

- 5 1/2 cups flour 780 grams
- four tablespoons of baking powder
- 1 teaspoon cinnamon
- 1/2 teaspoon of cinnamon
- two ounces of unsweetened cocoa powder 2/3 cup
- 1 pound almonds finely ground 3 1/2 cups
- 6 eggs extra-large, room temperature
- 1 pound of honey 1 1/3 cups, mildly heated
- 1 cup granulated sugar

- two oranges' zest
- the juice of one orange
- 1 teaspoon pure vanilla extract
- Excellent chocolate for glazing purposes. At least 70 percent bittersweet chocolate is my preference.

Instructions

1. Preheat oven 350 degrees F. Place rack in the middle.
2. Use parchment paper to line a baking sheet.
3. In a large mixing basin, sift dry ingredients together. (flour, baking powder, cinnamon, cocoa, and cloves).
4. Add ground almonds to the dry ingredients and combine. Set aside.
5. Beat the eggs for two to three minutes in a large mixing bowl or the whisk attachment's bowl.
6. Add honey. Continue whisking until the mixture is sufficiently thickened.
7. Add sugar. Beat effectively.
8. Add orange zest, orange juice, and orange extract.
9. Change to the paddle attachment. Add flour mixture until just mixed. (Dough will be sticky and soft.)
10. Working in small batches, place dough on a well-floured wooden board and roll to a thickness of 1/4 to 1/2 inch.
11. Cut dough into squares using a rhombus-shaped cutter or a knife (I use a 2-inch cutter).
12. Place on baking sheets.
13. Continue until the entirety of the dough has been molded. Trimmings of leftover dough can be re-rolled.

14.   Bake at 350 degrees Fahrenheit for 15 to 18 minutes, or until firm.

15.   Allow cooling completely before applying the chocolate glaze.

Chewy Italian Almond Cookies

servings: 20 cookies

calories: 128kcal

prep time:30 MINS

cook time:20 MINS

drying time:1 HR

total time:50 MINS

INGREDIENTS

- add two egg whites
- 1 dash of lemon juice
- 2 1/4 tablespoons almond flour
- 1 3/4 cups confectioners' sugar
- 1 pinch salt
- 1/4 tsp baking powder
- 1 tsp orange zest, or around half of a large orange
- 1 tbsp almond extract
- 1 tsp vanilla extract
- Use one-half cup powdered sugar to coat cookies.

INSTRUCTIONS

1. Using a stand mixer or hand mixer, whip egg whites and lemon juice until firm peaks form.

2. Using a sieve with a fine mesh, sift almond flour, 1 3/4 cups powdered sugar, salt, and baking powder into the egg whites, and then fold in. Not all at once, but perhaps in two or three bunches. Try to retain some air in the egg whites, although, at this time, the mixture will form a rather sticky dough, not a meringue.

3. Fold in orange zest, vanilla, and almond extract until thoroughly mixed.

4. Line a sheet pan with parchment paper. Roll dough into 1"-diameter balls using clean hands, then coat them thoroughly in powdered sugar. Form into an oval, then place on a baking sheet with space between them to allow for spreading and slightly flatten.

5. Leave at room temperature for approximately one hour or until the tops have formed a shell. (This may take more time in humid climates.) Before cracking the shell, gently squeeze the cookies from opposite corners. (Not doing so won't damage the flavor, but pre-cracking makes them much more attractive if you want that white-gold contrast!)

6. While the cookies dry, preheat the oven to 300 degrees. When the cookies are done, bake them for around twenty minutes. Refrigerate and place in an airtight container. These are even more delicious the next day and go well with coffee or tea!

The Best Italian Cream Cake

Prep Time: 30 minutes

Cook Time: 55 minutes

Total Time: 1 hour 25 minutes

Servings: 15

Ingredients

For the cake:

- 1/2 cup (1 stick) softened salted butter, at room temperature
- 1/2 cup vegetable margarine (CRISCO)
- 2 cups sugar
- 5 big egg yolks
- 1 cup buttermilk
- 1 teaspoon vanilla extract
- 1 teaspoon baking soda
- 2 cups all-purpose flour
- 1/2 cup of sweetened coconut flakes
- 1 cup ground walnuts
- 5 big egg whites beaten

For the garnish:

- 1/2 cup (1 stick) room-temperature salted butter
- An 8-ounce brick of room-temperature cream cheese
- 1 teaspoon vanilla extract
- 1 box of powdered sugar (16 ounces)
- For the topping, sweetened coconut shreds and chopped pecans

Instructions

For the topping:

1. Preheat oven to 325 °F. Coat a 9-by-13-inch baking dish with nonstick cooking spray.
2. In a large basin (or the stand of an electric mixer), combine butter, shortening, and sugar until smooth.

3. Add egg yolks one at a time, blending thoroughly after each addition with an electric hand mixer or stand mixer.

4. Combine buttermilk, vanilla extract, and baking soda in a small bowl.

5. Add half a cup of flour at a time and a quarter of the buttermilk mixture.

6. Repeat until all of the flour and buttermilk has been incorporated. When you add an ingredient, thoroughly blend it using a hand mixer or stand mixer.

7. Stir in the pecans, sweetened coconut, and gently beaten egg whites until thoroughly combined. Pour batter into a dish that has been prepared.

8. Bake for 40-45 minutes.

9. Reduce heat to 225 degrees Fahrenheit and bake for 10 minutes, or until a toothpick inserted in the center comes out clean. Allow cooling thoroughly.

For the garnish:

1. Combine butter, cream cheese, vanilla, and a quarter of the powdered sugar in a large bowl with an electric mixer.

2. Mix on high speed until smooth, then add additional powdered sugar. Continue until the box is empty and the frosting is perfectly smooth.

3. Frost and top the cooled cake with coconut and pecans, then serve.

Zeppole, Italian Ricotta Doughnuts

Prep Time15 minutes

Cook Time20 minutes

Servings20 doughnuts

Ingredients

- 3/4 cup plus 1 teaspoon all-purpose flour
- two tablespoons of baking powder
- grain of salt
- three tablespoons of powdered sugar
- 1 cup ricotta cheese (full fat)
- 2 big eggs
- canola oil
- sugar powder for dusting

Instructions

1. Sift the flour, baking powder, salt, and 3 tablespoons of sugar in a medium bowl.
2. In a stand mixer or hand-held mixer, combine the eggs and ricotta cheese until relatively smooth.
3. The flour mixture should be well incorporated into the ricotta mixture.
4. In a large, heavy pot or Dutch oven, pour enough oil to reach a depth of 2 inches and heat to 375 degrees F. A candy thermometer is useful for ensuring that the oil temperature does not drop below 350 degrees Fahrenheit between frying batches.
5. If the oil isn't hot enough, the doughnuts will be too mushy, and if it's too hot, the exterior will brown too rapidly, leaving the interior uncooked.
6. Put dough pieces into the hot oil using a 1 1/2-inch scoop or two small spoons.

7. Fry the zeppole for two to three minutes, flipping them frequently until they are golden and puffy.

8. Larger doughnuts will require additional cooking time. Remove the zeppole from the pan with a slotted spoon and drain them on paper towels. Continue until all batter is used.

9. Dust with confectioners' sugar or powdered sugar and serve warm.

Slow Cooker Tuscan White Bean Soup

Total: 8 hrs 45 mins

Hands-On:

15 mins

Yield: Serves 8

Ingredients

- 6 cups chicken stock, unsalted (such as Swanson)
- 1.5 cups minced onion
- 1 cup diced carrot
- 1 cup sliced celery
- 5 minced garlic cloves
- four fresh thyme leaves
- 1 bay leaf
- 1 pound of dried Great Northern beans
- 3 cups stemmed and sliced kale
- 2 tablespoons tomato paste without salt
- 38 teaspoon kosher salt
- 1 pound of links of hot Italian sausage, casings removed
- 2 teaspoons fresh lemon juice
- 1 ounce of shaved Parmesan cheese (about 1/4 cup).

Directions

1. Place the first eight ingredients in a 6-quart slow cooker. Cover and cook for 8 hours on LOW. Throw out the thyme and bay leaf.

2. Add the kale, tomato paste, and salt to the bean mixture. Form sausage into 32 meatballs, then place on the bean mixture. Cover and cook until the meatballs are cooked through. Stir in juice. Pour soup into eight bowls and top with cheese.

Italian Turkey and Orzo Soup

Yield: Serves 4 (serving size: about 2 cups)

Ingredients

- 1 tablespoon olive oil
- 12 ounces of ground turkey that is 93% lean
- 1 tablespoon of chopped fresh oregano
- 4 ounces cremini mushrooms, sliced
- 5 minced garlic cloves
- 3 cups chicken stock, unsalted (such as Swanson)
- 2 cups of water
- ½ teaspoon kosher salt
- 1/2 teaspoon red pepper powder
- 1 can of small diced tomatoes, 15 ounces, drained
- 3/4 cup uncooked orzo pasta made with whole wheat
- 3 cups spinach
- 1/2 teaspoon grated citrus peel

Directions

1. Bring a large Dutch oven to a medium-high temperature. Add oil; coat by swirling. Add turkey; heat for 6 minutes, frequently stirring, until lightly browned and crumbly. Oregano, mushrooms, and garlic are then sautéed for five minutes. Bring 2 cups water, salt, red pepper, and

tomatoes to a boiling stock, scraping pan to release browned pieces. Cook orzo for 7 minutes. Add spinach and zest; simmer for 2 minutes.

Italian Wedding Risotto Soup

Serves 4 (serving size: about 1 1/2 cups)

Ingredients

- 6 ounces of delicious Italian sausage in bulk
- 1 tablespoon canola oil
- one-half cup minced shallots
- 1 teaspoon chopped garlic
- 1/4 teaspoon red pepper powder
- 4 cups chicken stock, unsalted
- Reserve 1 1/2 cups of cooked risotto from the Sweet Onion Risotto with Sautéed Kale.
- 1 cup chopped escarole
- ¼ teaspoon kosher salt
- 1 ounce of shaved Parmesan cheese (about 1/4 cup).

Directions

1. Portion and form sausage into twenty-six balls (about 1 teaspoon each). Bring a large Dutch oven to a medium temperature. Add oil; whirl. Add shallots, garlic, and crushed red pepper and sauté for five minutes. Bring chicken stock to a boil before adding. Add reserved sausage and risotto from Sweet Onion Risotto with Sautéed Kale; decrease heat and simmer for 5 minutes. Add escarole and salt; simmer for two minutes. Distribute among four bowls; sprinkle with shaved Parmesan.

Slow Cooker Cioppino

Total:7 hrs 45 mins

Hands-On: 20 mins

Yield: Serves 4 (serving size: 2 cups)

Ingredients

- 2 tablespoons extra-virgin olive oil
- 1.5 cups minced onion
- 1 1/2 cups chopped bulb of fennel
- 10 chopped garlic cloves
- 1 cup of dry white wine
- two tablespoons of tomato paste
- half a cup of water
- 2 teaspoons fresh chopped oregano
- 2 teaspoons freshly chopped thyme
- 1/4 teaspoon red pepper powder
- .38 teaspoon kosher salt
- 1/2 pound fresh sliced tomatoes
- Two 2-inch slices of lemon rind
- 2 laurel leaves
- 1 (26-ounce) container of chopped tomatoes (such as Pom).
- 3/4 pounds of cod sliced into 2-inch lengths
- 1/2 pounds of sea scallops
- 1/2 pounds of medium peeled and deveined shrimp
- 1 tablespoon fresh lemon juice
- 1/4 cup of fresh basil

Directions

- Medium-heat a big skillet. Swirl oil. Add onion, fennel, and garlic to the pan; simmer until tender, approximately 3 minutes. Bring the wine and tomato paste to a boil, stirring well. Cook for two minutes, stirring intermittently.

- Pour the onion mixture with care into a 6-quart electric slow cooker. Add 1/2 cup water and the following eight ingredients (through tomato paste) to the slow cooker. Cook covered on LOW for 7 hours.

- Remove the lid and discard the lemon peel and bay leaves. Add cod, scallops, shrimp, and lemon juice to the pan. Cover and simmer on LOW heat for 13 to 15 minutes, or until the salmon flakes easily with a fork. Garnish with basil leaves.

Christmas Soup

PREP TIME5 mins

COOK TIME2 hrs

TOTAL TIME2 hrs 5 mins

SERVINGS6 people

INGREDIENTS

- 1 14.5-ounce can of chopped tomatoes with juice

- 1 14.5-ounce can of Italian stewed tomatoes in their juice

- 1 ten-ounce can of Rotel Original tomatoes and green chilies with the liquid

- 1 pound of Velveeta cheese cut into 1-inch thick slices

- 4 cup vegetable stock or chicken stock

- 1 cup sour cream

- 1 12-ounce box of tricolor spiral-shaped pasta cooked 30 seconds BELOW al dente according to package instructions.

- 1 tablespoon coarsely chopped fresh basil
- scoops tortilla chips
- Sprinkle crushed red pepper flakes on top

INSTRUCTIONS

1. In a slow cooker, combine the tomatoes and their liquid. Using a spoon, cut the stewed tomatoes into pieces.
2. Add the chicken stock and Velveeta. 1 hour on high heat.
3. Stir in the sour cream.
4. Add cooked pasta and basil to the pan.
5. Cook for one hour on high to thicken the soup. (see Notes)
6. Serve garnished with red pepper flakes, more basil, and tortilla chips.

NOTES

- Once the pasta is added, the broth will get thicker. After one hour, the consistency is just right — neither too thick nor too thin. You can continue cooking in the slow cooker for another hour or two, but drop the heat to low before adding the pasta. Otherwise, the soup will become more like cheese than soup. In addition, pasta can overcook if left in the slow cooker for more than an hour.
- In the absence of a slow cooker, this soup may be prepared just as quickly on the stovetop. Melt the cheese over medium heat while stirring often in the first two steps. Reduce heat to low and continue with the remaining stages.
- Calorie estimation does not include tortilla chips.

Instant Pot Christmas Soup

Prep Time: 10 minutes

Cook Time: 0 minute pressure cook time

Yield: 8–10 servings 1x

Ingredients

- 7 cups poultry or vegetable stock
- One (14.5-ounce) can of tiny chopped tomatoes in juice
- 1 (14.5 oz) can of Italian tomato sauce with the juice
- 1 (10-ounce) can of Rotel Original tomatoes with green chilies and juice
- 1 (12-ounce) bag of spiral-shaped pasta in three colors
- 16 ounce Velveeta cheese
- 1/4 cup milk
- tablespoon fresh basil
- A pinch of red pepper

Instructions

Instructions for the Instant Pot:

1. Sauté broth in the Instant Pot. Allow the broth to reheat while you prepare the remaining ingredients.
2. Add diced tomatoes, Italian tomatoes, and Rotel tomatoes to the dish. Place the spaghetti and Velveeta in the pot.
3. Turn off the saute function. Securely cover Instant Pot with the lid. Ensure the valve is adjusted to seal. Adjust the soup's timer to 0 minutes (yes, zero).
4. After the time has elapsed, allow the pot to rest for five minutes before alternating the valve between sealing and venting until no foam escapes. Turn the venting valve to discharge all pressure. Take off the lid.
5. Mix milk, basil, and cayenne pepper into the soup.
6. Pour the soup into dishes and serve.
7. Place broth, all of the tomatoes, Velveeta, and pasta into the slow cooker.

8. Cover and simmer on high for 2 to 3 hours, or until the pasta is fully cooked. (Every slow cooker is different)
9. Mix in the milk, basil, and cayenne pepper.
10. Pour the soup into dishes and serve.

Notes

This soup is best served immediately since the pasta will absorb the broth and become a pasta dish rather than a soup.

Easy Christmas Appetizer "Hummus Wreath"

yield: 1 APPETIZER PLATTER

prep time: 10 MINUTES

total time: 10 MINUTES

Ingredients

- 1 (17-ounce) jar of plain hummus (we use "Classic" from Sabra) (or use your favorite homemade)
- 1/2 cup of crumbled, reduced-fat feta cheese
- 1/4 cup green onions finely sliced (from about 2 onions)
- 3/4 cup minced flat-leaf Italian parsley
- 1 teaspoon virgin extra olive oil
- 1/16 teaspoon kosher salt
- halved cherry tomatoes (I used four and a half tomatoes for the wreath depicted in this post).
- optional 1 big red pepper (look for one with broad, flat sides)
- 1 to 1 1/2 tablespoons of reduced-fat, coarsely shredded feta cheese

- Optional dipping accompaniments: whole-grain pita chips, whole-wheat pita bread wedges, or red and green vegetables

Instructions

1. Mix hummus, 1/2 cup feta, and green onions.

2. Place a small dish or glass in the middle of a 12.5-inch-diameter platter. If you intend to add a bowl of pita chips or vegetables in the center of the finished wreath (like we did in several of our photographs), you will need to use that bowl (or a similarly sized glass) to ensure that the hole in the center of the wreath is the correct size. Use a rubber scraper to spread the hummus mixture in a circular pattern around the bowl/glass in the center (refer to the photos in our post to see how we did this). Remove the bowl/glass from the middle by gently twisting it upward. If necessary, you can delicately put the tip of a toothpick under the bowl or glass's rim to assist with its release.

3. In a small bowl, combine parsley, oil, and salt until the parsley is equally covered and the oil and salt are dispersed evenly. Spoon the parsley mixture in a circular pattern on top of the hummus, leaving a little border of hummus visible all around.

4. Distribute cherry tomato halves, cut-side down, among the parsley layer to resemble Christmas ornaments.

5. If constructing the optional bow from red pepper, cut one broad, flat side off the pepper (as indicated in the photo in our post) and press a bow-shaped cookie cutter (we use this one) gently but firmly through the pepper slice to cut out the bow. Attach the bow to the wreath.

6. To simulate snow, carefully dust the entire wreath with 1 to 1 1/2 tablespoons of very finely crushed feta. Depending on the width of your

wreath, you can vary the exact amount of feta; you want it to resemble a light dusting, but not so much that it obscures the other ingredients.

7. Serve immediately with your preferred dipping accompaniments, or cover and refrigerate for 1–2 days. (See preparation tips below.)

Notes

Make-ahead tips: This recipe can be partially prepared in advance by combining the ingredients for the humus and the parsley salad layers; chill them separately until ready to assemble the wreath. Alternately, you can prepare the entire wreath up to one or two days in advance. Wrap the plate tightly in plastic wrap and refrigerate it, ensuring that the wrap does not adhere to or damage the wreath. Also, note that preparing the parsley layer in advance may soften and darken a little, but it will still look wonderful and taste delicious.

Easy antipasto wreath

Prep Time: 20 minutes

Cook Time: 0 minutes

Total Time: 20 minutes

Servings: 8

Ingredients

For the marinated mozzarella

- 200 g bocconcini/mozzarella balls
- ¼ cup olive oil
- 1 lemon juiced
- 2 smashed garlic cloves
- 2 teaspoons chopped parsley

- 1 tsp dried oregano
- pepper and salt to taste
- two hundred grams of salami or prosciutto
- 2 cups artichokes marinated
- 3 tablespoons pickled peppers
- 1 cup of fresh green olives
- 1 cup Kalamata olives
- 2 cups Cherry tomatoes
- crostini
- rosemary to build the wreath's foundation

Instructions

1. To marinate the mozzarella, combine the marinade ingredients, add the cheese, and let it marinate for 10 minutes.

2. Place the rosemary in a circle on a big dish, then add the cheese that has been marinated, pickled, and marinated vegetables, meat, and olives. Serve the remaining marinade drizzled over the meat.

CHRISTMAS ANTIPASTO PLATTER

PREP TIME: 20 minutes

COOK TIME: 0 minutes

TOTAL TIME: 20 minutes

YIELD: 8 servings 1x

INGREDIENTS

- Eight ounces of smoked pepper-jack cheese, sliced and then cut into triangles
- 8 ounces of salami, sliced
- 1 pound grape halved if on the bigger side, sliced in half

- A one-pound package of green, black, or a combination of the two marinated olives
- 1 pound balls of fresh mozzarella
- Sweety Drop Peppers weighing 8 ounces
- 8 ounces of tapenade made from olives
- offering crackers or crostini
- rosemary used as a garnish
- 10 Pomegranate seeds used as a garnish
- One yellow bell pepper, sliced into the shape of a star, for the tree's top.

INSTRUCTIONS

1. Remove a strip from the pepper's flat side. Use a kitchen cutter in the shape of a star to cut the pepper, or use a knife and cut it by hand.
2. Assemble the ingredients into a Christmas tree-shaped triangle and top with fresh rosemary sprigs.
3. Serve with your choice of crostini or crackers.

RECIPE NOTES

- If Sweety Drop peppers are unavailable, substitute roasted red peppers, spicy cherry peppers, or sliced bell peppers.
- The nutritional information is for all of the foods on the platter, divided equally, excluding crackers; the nutritional value could be greater or lower depending on what you consume.

Prosciutto, Brie and Arugula Bruschetta

Prep Time 10 mins

Cook Time 6 mins

Ingredients

- 6 pieces of fresh baguette
- 200 grams of sliced and rind-free brie
- six slices of dry-cured prosciutto
- 5 tbsp. olive oil extra virgin
- a handful of fresh arugula
- 2 tsp toasted pine nuts (optional)
- Balsamic Vinaigrette (optional)
- ¼ cup olive oil extra virgin
- 2 tbsp. balsamic vinegar

Instructions

1. Preheat oven 200 degrees 400 degrees F and line a medium-sized baking sheet with baking paper.
2. Cut baguette diagonally into six 14"-thick slices. Oil one side of each slice.
3. Heat a saucepan or skillet over medium heat. Toast each baguette slice with the oiled side facing down for 1 to 2 minutes, until aromatic and gently browned on the bottom. Transfer bread to a baking sheet with the toasted side up.
4. Remove rind from brie and slice cheese thinly. Place one to two cheese slices on each slice of the toasted baguette. Each piece of bread must be covered with brie.
5. Bake for 3 to 5 minutes in a preheated oven until the brie barely begins to melt. Cool in oven. Add sliced prosciutto, fresh arugula, and toasted

pine nuts on top (optional). Drizzle olive oil or balsamic vinaigrette over the salad (see below).

6. To Make Balsamic Vinaigrette: Mix olive oil and balsamic vinegar in a bowl, then drizzle over bruschetta.

Italian Black Pepper Cookies

PREP TIME20 mins

COOK TIME20 mins

TOTAL TIME40 mins

SERVINGS24

INGREDIENTS

- 2 cups all-purpose flour
- 1 teaspoon of baking powder
- ½ teaspoon salt
- 2 tablespoons black pepper coarsely ground
- half a cup of water
- ½ cup olive oil
- olive oil for brushing;
- 8. 2 tablespoons of granulated sugar OPTIONAL

INSTRUCTIONS

1. First, combine the dry ingredients in a large bowl. Create a well in the center for the liquid components.

2. Pour the water and oil slowly into the flour's well. Using your hands, gradually integrate the mixture into the flour. The dough will be substantial.

3. Sprinkle flour on a work surface or cutting board. Knead the dough for approximately three minutes to generate the gluten.

4. Preheat oven to 400 degrees.

5. Tear tablespoon-sized pieces of dough. Next, roll into extremely thin, 6-inch-long ropes.

6. Form a ring before pinching the edges together.

7. Spray or grease a baking pan. Leave room between each Tarallo, as they will not expand significantly but will increase slightly.

8. Each baking sheet may accommodate 12 cookies. You may bake one at a time or both at once; simply rotate the pans halfway through and keep them close to the oven's center.

9. Brush with oil and bake in the center of the oven for twenty minutes. The bottoms will be toasted lightly.

10. Remove the cookies off the baking sheet with care and allow them to cool on a cooling rack.

11. Consume immediately as an appetizer, snack, or small bite. Serve alongside wine or small nibbles such as cheese, fruit, or salumi. Excellent for serving on a cheeseboard or in a breadbasket.

Crescent Roll Wreaths

YIELD: 6 WREATHS

PREP TIME10 minutes

COOK TIME12 minutes

TOTAL TIME22 minutes

Ingredients

- 1 packet dough sheet for crescent rolls
- 2 teaspoons butter, melted
- 1 teaspoon Italian spices
- 1 teaspoon minced garlic
- 2 fresh rosemary sprigs
- Two slices of cheddar

Instructions

1. Preheat the oven to 375 °F and line a baking sheet with parchment paper.
2. Cut the sheet of crescent roll dough into six 2-inch-wide strips.
3. Cut the strip lengthwise along the middle, leaving the strip's end intact.
4. Twist the two strips together until they reach the end, then bring the ends together to form a circle at the top.
5. Place the crescent roll wreaths on the baking sheet lined with parchment paper and brush with melted butter.
6. Add Italian spice and garlic powder to each one.
7. Bake the crescent rolls in a preheated oven for 9 to 12 minutes, or until golden brown.
8. Once the rolls have cooled, cut the rosemary sprigs into six pieces and set one on top of each wreath.
9. Use a small star-shaped cookie cutter to cut out star shapes from the cheese slices, then place one star on each wreath.

Best Italian Stuffed Artichokes

Prep Time: 30 minutes

Cook Time: 30 minutes

Total Time: 1 hour

Servings: 12

Ingredients

- 2 cups of toasted bread crumbs
- 2 tsp Sicilian Spice blend.
- 4 cloves of Garlic
- 6 tablespoons Extra virgin olive oil (we used Norcellara Organic Reserve EVOO by Mie Radici)
- 1/3 cup grated Parmesan cheese
- 1/4 cup finely minced Parsley
- "Season with salt and pepper to taste."
- 3 giant artichokes (our artichokes had a diameter of 6 inches (15 cm) and were enormous) Globe Artichokes
- 1 Lemon juice of one lemon

Instructions

Prepare the filling:

1. Combine toasted bread crumbs, Sicilian spice blend, fresh minced garlic, extra virgin olive oil, parmesan cheese, minced parsley, and salt & pepper to taste in a medium bowl. (You may instead use Italian toasted bread crumbs that have already been blended and omit the Sicilian Spice Blend.) Set Aside.

2. Clean the artichokes. Remove the stem from the bottom of the artichoke so it may sit flat on the table. Set stems aside. To avoid oxidation, rub the bottom of the artichoke with the lemon half and sprinkle with lemon juice.

3. Remove the lowest two to three rows of leaves from the artichoke using your hands. They should be easily detachable. Using a pair of sharp kitchen shears, remove the pointy tip of the leaves (about 14 inches). The reason for removing them is that they can be unpleasant when consumed. Thus, they must be eliminated. To avoid oxidation, cover artichokes in lemon juice.

4. Then, place the artichoke on its side and, using a sharp knife, trim off the top 1 inch of leaves. Keep the choke in place. Do not remove it. The artichoke stalks are peeled. To avoid oxidation, artichokes and stems should be rubbed with lemon.

5. Next, carefully stretch the artichoke's ends to make space for the Italian filling. Gently draw back each leaf and place a small amount of stuffing in each leaf and a small amount on top. Drizzle with a small amount of extra virgin olive oil.

6. Find a large and deep saucepan to hold your artichokes and has a tight-fitting lid for stovetop steaming. You can utilize a steaming basket within the pot, crisscrossed chopsticks and a plate, steamer oven technology, or a bamboo steamer. Fill bottom of the pot with enough water to reach 2 inches up the pot's side. Put the lid on the pot and steam the artichokes for about 25 to 30 minutes, or until a knife can easily pierce the bottom of the artichoke's heart. Your steaming time will depend on the size of your artichokes and the vessel you use. (Please observe the water level in your pot closely. Adding additional water may be necessary throughout the steaming process. Don't let your pot go dry)

Method using an Instant Pot/Pressure Cooker:

1. After cleaning, drizzling with lemon juice, preparing, and stuffing your artichokes, put one and a half cups of water in the bottom of your instant pot. Place the Instant Pot's included basket inside the Instant Pot. Place the stuffed artichokes on top of the basket and secure the cover. Depending on the size of your artichokes, set the instant pot to steam (High pressure) for 9 to 12 minutes. Use NOT the rapid steam release feature. Use the natural self-release method instead, as this will continue cooking the artichokes. Three huge globe artichokes were present in our 6-quart instant pot. We cooked three huge stuffed globe artichokes for 11 minutes, delightfully tender. We employed the natural release approach for steaming.

2. You can serve Your Best Italian Stuffed Artichokes warm or at room temperature. Best consumed within three days. In the refrigerator, leftovers can be stored in a sealed container.

How to eat artichokes packed with cheese:

1. Start by removing the outer leaves, place each leaf individually in your mouth and scrape the delicate stuffing and artichoke meat between your teeth. This should keep you busy for a while, as there are around four layers of leaves to remove. Stop removing the leaves if their color begins to lighten and they develop a purple margin. You are nearing the choke point. Avoid eating this portion. Instead, scrape the purple and light-colored leaves and the prickly choke using a spoon. Because the steaming softens this area, it can be easily scraped off. Only the valuable artichoke heart will remain after discarding the choke and choke leaves. The artichoke heart should be soft enough to cut with a fork. Enjoy! Chow!

Notes

- To prevent oxidation and browning of the leaves, sprinkle fresh lemon juice over the chopped artichokes.
- Use gluten-free bread crumbs if you wish to prepare gluten-free food. To make vegan, substitute parmesan with nutritional yeast.

Caponata alla Siciliana

PREP TIME10 mins

COOK TIME25 mins

TOTAL TIME35 mins

SERVINGS6

EQUIPMENT

Lidded sauté pan

INGREDIENTS

- 1 tablespoon olive oil
- 1 eggplant aubergine
- 1 zucchini courgette
- two diced celery sticks
- 1 sliced red onion
- 2 minced garlic cloves
- 14 ounces 400 gram can of diced tomatoes
- 1 teaspoon drained capers
- 10 olives, green or black, pitted and quartered
- 1 teaspoon of red wine vinegar
- 1 teaspoon of granulated sugar
- 1 tbsp optionally shredded dark chocolate

TO SERVE:

- 1 baguette

- 1 clove of garlic, cut in half

- fresh basil in tiny sprigs or finely minced

- Extra virgin olive oil

INSTRUCTIONS

1. First, dice the eggplant and zucchini (no need to peel).

2. Heat the oil in a big skillet, then sauté the eggplant and zucchini for 5 minutes, or until tender. Depending on the size of your pan, cook in batches. Remove and set aside the eggplant and zucchini.

3. Add the celery, onion, and garlic to the pan without first cleaning it, and simmer for a few minutes, until tender but not browned.

4. Add tomatoes, capers, olives, sugar, vinegar, and chocolate. Season with pepper (there is already salt from the capers and olives) and bring to a boil, then reduce heat and toss in the eggplant and zucchini that have been cooked. Cover the pan with a lid and cook, stirring regularly, for 15 minutes.

5. To serve as an appetizer, slice the baguette into 14-inch thick slices, toast each side, and sprinkle each slice with a clove of garlic that has been sliced in half. Warm or cold, top each slice with a tablespoon of the caponata, a basil sprig, and a drizzle of oil. The caponata should not be added until just before serving.

NOTES

If preparing bruschetta or crostini, do not add the caponata until before serving.

Antipasto Wreath

Prep Time20 mins

Total Time20 mins

Servings: 10

Ingredients

- 1 (8 oz) jar of small fresh mozzarella balls
- 2 pints of cherry tomatoes
- 1 (15 oz) container of quartered artichoke hearts in the marinade
- 1 (12-ounce) container of chopped roasted red peppers
- black olives
- 6 slices salami
- 6 slices prosciutto
- 6 slices capicola
- 4 halved sweet or spicy cherry peppers
- aromatic basil
- sprigs of fresh rosemary

Instructions

1. Artichoke hearts, black olives, roasted red peppers, cherry peppers, and mozzarella balls should be drained of their juices and oils. Arrange ingredients in dishes
2. On each toothpick, skewer three things plus fresh basil leaves. Mix and match the ingredients on each skewer so that each is unique.
3. Place toothpicks in the shape of a wreath on a big round plate, stacking them two to three layers high.

4. Place rosemary sprigs on top of your wreath and nestled in throughout, ensuring that they protrude slightly to simulate the wreath's foliage.

5. In a ramekin or small bowl, add a balsamic glaze or Italian dressing to the center of the wreath.

Air Fryer Mozzarella Sticks

PREP TIME15 mins

COOK TIME10 mins

ADDITIONAL TIME2 hrs

TOTAL TIME2 hrs 25 mins

SERVINGS16 Pieces

INGREDIENTS

- 8 string cheese sticks I like the low-fat version of this recipe over the full-fat version.
- 1/3 cup all-purpose flour
- 1/2 teaspoon paprika
- 2 teaspoons of dried oregano
- 2 teaspoons of fresh parsley
- 1 teaspoon minced garlic
- 1 teaspoon powdered onion
- 1/2 teaspoon salt
- 1/2 cup panko breadcrumbs
- 1 egg

INSTRUCTIONS

1. Putting Together The Mozzarella Cheese Sticks

2. Cut each cheese stick in half to yield 16 equal pieces.

3. Combine panko, paprika, oregano, parsley, garlic powder, onion powder, and salt in a small bowl.

4. Add one egg to a second small bowl and beat it with a fork (or whisk).

5. Add the flour to the third small bowl.

6. Using a fork, dunk each piece of cheese in the flour, the egg, and finally the panko and spice combination. Once coated, transfer to a baking sheet. I prefer to line the baking pan with parchment paper to facilitate cleanup.

7. Continue coating all cheese cubes and arranging them on the baking sheet.

8. Place cheese sticks in the freezer for at least two hours or until completely frozen. The cheese sticks can then be placed in a freezer bag for storage or air frying.

9. Cheese Sticks Prepared in an Air Fryer

10. Set the air fryer to 400 degrees F. Allow reheating for one or two minutes until warm.

11. Spray the air fryer basket with a fine mist of oil facing away from the air fryer machine to prevent oil from reaching the heating element.

12. Add frozen mozzarella cheese sticks to the air fryer basket so that they are not touching in a single layer. (I could fit seven to eight in my basket)

13. Heat cheese sticks for three to four minutes, then remove them from the air fryer and shake or turn them with tongs. Cook for 3 to 4 minutes on the other side, or until brown, crispy, and juicy. If they aren't quite crispy enough, simply bake them for an extra minute.

14.   Serve while still hot with marinara for dipping!

ITALIAN STUFFED MUSHROOMS

Prep Time20 mins

Cook Time15 mins

Total Time35 mins

Servings: 24 mushrooms

INGREDIENTS

- 24 button mushrooms with stems removed, cleaned, and dried
- 1 minced clove of garlic
- 1/4 cup seasoned Italian bread crumbs
- 1/4 cup shredded mozzarella cheese
- 2 tablespoons of grated Parmesan cheese
- 1 tsp dried parsley
- 3 tbsps butter, melted
- 1/4 tsp table salt
- cooking spray

INSTRUCTIONS

1. Preheat oven to 425 degrees F.
2. To prepare mushrooms, remove the stems and wash and dry the caps.
3. In a small bowl, combine the remainder of the ingredients. Stuff the mushrooms and lay them on a cooking spray-coated baking sheet with a rim.
4. Bake for fifteen minutes, then serve immediately.

Ingredients

- 1 little egg white (about 3/4 ounce)
- 3/4 ounces simple syrup
- 1-ounce lemon juice
- 1 ½ ounce Ramazzotti Amaro
- ½ ounce El Dorado 5-year rum
- bitters of Angostura, for garnish

Method

All components should be combined in a cocktail shaker. Add three or four large ice cubes and shake briefly but thoroughly. Strain drinks from the large tin into the tiny tin for a reverse dry shake and discard ice. Again, shake without ice for 10 to 15 seconds to form a meringue. Pour into a chilled coupe glass and add a dash of Angostura bitters.

Very Berry Light

Ingredients

- 2 blackberries, divided
- 3 raspberries, divided
- 75 ounces Italicus Bergamot Oil
- 3 ounces of white Chenin Blanc wine
- three drops of white wine vinegar

Method

One blackberry and two raspberries are softly crushed in a cocktail shaker. Add ice, Italics, white wine, and vinegar. Shake, then filter twice into a wine glass. Skewer the remaining blackberries and raspberries for garnish.

Babbo's Toddy

INGRADIENTS

- Cinnamon Syrup
- 14 grams of cinnamon bark
- 5 L water
- 5 L sugar
- 1-ounce sweet vermouth
- 5-ounce bourbon
- 5 ounce Campari
- 75 ounces cinnamon syrup
- Boiling water
- Wheel of orange, for garnish

Method

To prepare the cinnamon syrup:

1. Bring water and cinnamon to a boil and then simmer for twenty minutes.
2. Turn off the heat.
3. After straining cinnamon sticks, add sugar.
4. Stir thoroughly.

5. In a toddy mug or tumbler that has been heated, add the vermouth, bourbon, Campari, and cinnamon syrup separately. Fill the remaining space with hot water and decorate with an orange wheel.

Grampa Joe

- Famous Grouse Blended Scotch, 1 oz and 1/2 ounce Punt E Mes
- 1/2 ounce Don Ciccio Ambrosia
- 1 teaspoon of coffee liqueur, Caffe Moka preferred
- Citrus twist as garnish
- Sea salt, as a condiment

Method

Combine all components except lemon and sea salt in a rock glass. Add ice and whisk vigorously for eight seconds. The oil extracted from the lemon peel is then used as a garnish. Sprinkle ice with a generous amount of salt.

Amaro Nog

- Amari Blend
- 25-ounce Meletti
- 25 oz Montenegro
- 25 oz Vallet Ango
- 25 Angostura
- 25 Cynar
- 75 Old Forester Rye

- 2 dashes of salt tincture (combine 1/8 teaspoon of sea salt and 1 tablespoon of boiling water).

Method

Mix all items and whisk carefully. Set aside.

Dark Hearts

- 1 ounce of Maker's Mark
- 75-ounce blackstrap rum.
- 5 ounce Fernet Vallet
- 5-ounce grenadine
- 5oz lemon
- Pomegranate seeds are used as a garnish

Method

In a cocktail shaker, combine all components except the pomegranate seeds. Stir quickly, then strain over crushed ice. Sprinkle pomegranate seeds on top.

Coffee & Cream

- 0.75 oz. brandy
- Mr. Black Cold Brew Coffee Liqueur, 0.75 ounce
- 0.175 oz. Vin Santo
- 1 oz. espresso
- 2 oz. hot water
- 0.75 oz. vanilla cream
- Cocoa powder, for embellishment

- Pollen is used as a garnish

Method

Create and layer the drink in a 6-ounce glass with a foot by adding each component without swirling. Then, decorate with cocoa powder and bee pollen.

Fireside Aperitivo

- 1 oz Pimm's 5 oz Campari
- 5 oz Meyer lemon juice or ordinary lemon juice
- 25 ounces of simple syrup
- Birra Moretti or an additional Italian lager
- Citrus slice used as a garnish
- Blood orange segment used as a garnish
- Sage leaves are used as a garnish

Method

Shake the Pimm's Campari, lemon juice, and simple syrup in a cocktail shaker. Strain twice into a Collins glass filled with ice. Add some Birra Moretti. Grapefruit, blood orange, and sage leaves serve as garnishes.

Made in United States
North Haven, CT
17 December 2024